THE JESUS PRAYER

Gospel Soundings

SISTER PAULINE MARGARET CHN

SLG Press
Convent of the Incarnation Fairacres
Parker Street Oxford OX4 1TB England

www.slgpress.co.uk

THE JESUS PRAYER

Gospel Soundings

ISBN   978-0-7283-0173-3
ISSN   0307-1405

Printed by Will Print Oxford England

CONTENTS

PREFACE

From the shelf in the Novitiate Room I picked up a little booklet. I was a very new member of my Community, whose full dedication was 'The Community of the Mission Sisters of the Holy Name of Jesus', and here was a book about praying by calling on the name of Jesus, *The Invocation of the Name of Jesus*, by a monk of the Eastern Church.

As I began to read, something tugged at my memory. It has always been curiously important to me that the church where I was baptised as a baby was (unusually) dedicated, not to a saint but simply to Jesus: 'Jesus Church, Forty Hill'. As I went on reading, I had an odd sense that I had stumbled on my spiritual home.

Forty years on, I can look back thankfully to that discovery on the bookshelf. Later, with gratitude, I found other encouraging teachers, Per Olaf Sjogren, Simon Barrington-Ward, Kallistos Ware, and others.

A teacher by training and by nature, I invariably discover my way to God through the discipline of getting ideas into words to which others can relate. The following reflections are the fruit of sharing my thoughts in Retreats, Prayer Workshops, Quiet Days. The response I experienced encouraged me to collect these reflections together in the hope that others might come to appreciate the richness of this simple approach to prayer. I am grateful for the encouragement and help of my Community and friends while the final version was shaping up, and to SLG Press for such a positive response to my enquiry about the possibility of publishing.

The 'Jesus Prayer' has always been for me a good place to start from when discouraged or lost in the dark on the spiritual pilgrimage. It has not been my only way of prayer, but it has been something I invariably come home to. In Chapter 10 of St John's Gospel, we read the words, they 'will come in and go out and find pasture'. Jesus is speaking of the 'fold' of the Good Shepherd. I like to apply the words to my experience of the Jesus Prayer. It is a home to come into and to go out from, a home for the 'travelling Christian'.

SISTER PAULINE MARGARET

COMMUNITY OF THE HOLY NAME

NOTE ON THE JESUS PRAYER

The invocation of the name of Jesus in prayer is often referred to as 'the Jesus Prayer'. It can simply be the attentive repetition of the name itself, 'Jesus, Jesus, Jesus, Jesus', or a longer form, including phrases deriving from the New Testament, such as:

'You are the Messiah,
the Son of the living God.' (Matthew 16: 16).

'Son of David, have mercy on me!' (Mark 10: 48).

'God, be merciful to me, a sinner!' (Luke 18: 13).

Forms of the prayer in frequent use are 'Lord Jesus Christ, have mercy' or 'Jesus, mercy', or the full version:

'Lord Jesus Christ, Son of God,
have mercy on me a sinner.'

INTRODUCTION

Professionals and amateurs

I have sometimes been impatient that, as a Sister belonging to a religious community, I am often allotted the statutory slot on 'prayer' at a conference or a training weekend. We are sometimes pigeon-holed as the 'professionals' at prayer. But of course this is nonsense. In ordinary terms, the amateur, as contrasted with the professional, is one who practises for love (literally, amateur equals lover!), rather than for a living. In that sense, we are all amateurs as well as professionals; we all practise prayer both for our living and for love. So, it is as an amateur professional that I write my own reflections on the Jesus Prayer.

The Lord's Prayer

The primary teaching of Jesus about prayer in the Gospels is the Lord's Prayer, the 'Our Father'. Jesus teaches his disciples to come to God in prayer in the relationship of the son or daughter to the Father; to come seeking God's honour, hallowing his name, longing for the coming of his kingdom and the fulfilling of God's purposes on earth, as in heaven; to come trusting in his providence, asking for our daily bread; to come acknowledging our need of forgiveness, salvation and deliverance.

In all this, Jesus is inviting his disciples to come to the Father through him, as St John's Gospel puts it. He is opening to his disciples the close relationship of communion which he himself enjoys, the 'Abba' relationship. We can trust that as he prayed, so he invites us to pray in and through him, to pray 'Abba'. The prayer itself is both the expression of and the journey toward our call and destiny to become like Christ, and in Christ to become renewed in the image and likeness of God.

Knowing God in Jesus

The spirituality of the Jesus Prayer is not an alternative to the spirituality of the Lord's Prayer; it is certainly not a higher level of spirituality. Rather, it can be understood as one way of entering into and of nurturing that communion and relationship with Jesus which enables and qualifies us to call God 'Father', and to pray as Jesus prayed.

> All things have been handed over to me by my Father, and no one knows the Son except the Father, and no one knows the Father except the Son and anyone to whom the Son chooses to reveal him.   Matthew 11: 27

In the Bible, the concept of *knowing* either God or another human being is not about factual, objective information but about intimate, intuitive empathy and experiential understanding. So it is not surprising that there arose in the traditions of Christianity a practice of not only praying to the Father through the Son, but of prayer to Jesus, seeking communion with Jesus in the intimacy of conversation and companionship and silent adoration.

The Jesus Prayer

As early Christians sought to grow in prayer and communion with Christ, they were often influenced by St Paul's injunction to 'pray at all times' (see I Thess. 5: 17 and Eph. 6: 18). As one response to this there grew up, primarily in the Eastern Churches of Greece and Russia, the 'Jesus Prayer'. In Western Christendom, although there has been no systematically taught practice of the invocation of the name of Jesus, nevertheless we find much evidence in the history of spirituality that a devotion to the name of Jesus has been practised and taught by many saints and spiritual teachers. Some of our best-loved hymns reflect this tradition:

'How sweet the Name of Jesus sounds', is one such, and

'Jesu the very thought of thee, with its verse:

Nor voice can sing, no heart can frame,
　　Nor can the memory find,
A sweeter sound than thy blest name,
　　O Saviour of mankind![1]

So, although it is the churches of the Eastern Orthodox tradition who give us the strongest and most systematic teaching about the Jesus Prayer, it is by no means alien to western spirituality.

It is in that confidence that I dare to write my own amateur reflections on the Jesus Prayer, although I am not a member of the Orthodox tradition.

---

[1] Latin c. twelfth century, tr. Edward Caswall, (1814-78), *The New English Hymnal*, the Canterbury Press Norwich, 1994.

USING THE JESUS PRAYER

'With the mind in the heart'

In using the Jesus Prayer, we seek to pray (as Orthodox teaching expresses it) 'with the mind in the heart'. The 'heart' here denotes the centre of our being, the seat of our personhood in which God is present—God who created us, and who constantly seeks to renew us in his image and likeness. So the heart, in this teaching, is not so much our *emotional* centre as the God-given source of our being, God's life in our deepest heart. And 'mind' is not only our intellectual capacity to reason, but all the faculties of thought, imagination, intuition, sensing.

So we pray with the desire that all these faculties be drawn into the centre of our being. It is perhaps a bit like the centre of gravity in a circling world: all the activities on the surface are to be drawn in by prayerful attention to a centredness, a stillness of focus, where the touch of the creator God can be known in silence and in an immediacy of attention. One means of this prayerful attention is the steady, rhythmic repetition of a short phrase or 'prayer'.

In the full version of the Jesus Prayer, 'Lord, Jesus Christ, Son of God, have mercy on me a sinner', there are twelve words in all, and repeating these or shorter versions of the prayer can be a means of co-operating with the pull of the gravity toward our heart or deepest centre. In a kind of paradox, this co-operation can turn us inside out, from self-attention and self-centredness, to self-emptying attention to the 'beyond' in our midst; attention to the transcendent God who, though he is in all he has made, cannot be contained by his creation but is both 'other' and 'holy'.

Repetition of the Jesus Prayer, as with the attentive repetition of any short phrase from Scripture, is far from being 'vain' or 'empty' repetition. The words are not a magic formula, but a theological summary of our faith and trust in the incarnate Son of God. The words are filled with significance and richness for those who have frequently studied and reflected on their meaning. In the actual time of attentive prayer, the one praying is advised not to be thinking about the meaning of the words, but simply attending to the person and presence of Jesus. The theology behind the words has a richness which will enhance that attention and enrich the loving desire with which the words are repeated. So if I use the name of Jesus in prayer, I use it in the knowledge that 'Jesus' was and is the human name given to God's Son.

We are, of course, all different. God made each of us unique and each has a unique relationship with God and a unique path to God in prayer. The method of repetition to assist attention in prayer may or may not be of help to you. It is classic and good advice to 'pray as you can, not as you can't', but whatever is or is not helpful in the actual time of prayer, the following reflections are offered as an exploration of the theology and spirituality behind and within the words of the prayer in the hope that, in some way or other, they can be encouraging and helpful in deepening your relationship with God.

THE HEART OF THE PRAYER

The Name of Jesus

'Jesus' was and is the human name given to the incarnate Son of God, and to invoke the name of Jesus in prayer is to bring our understanding of who Jesus is into our approach to God and into the growth of our relationship and friendship with God.

In St Matthew's Gospel we read that the angel instructed Joseph, 'You shall call his name Jesus, for he will save his people from their sins.' This reminds us of the Hebrew meaning of the name Joshua, of which *Jesus* is the Greek form. *Joshua* means 'God Saves'. It seems that in New Testament times the Greek form, *Jesus,* was a fairly common name. We meet it elsewhere in the Bible: for example, *Jesus Ben Sirach,* (after whom the apocryphal book, Ecclesiasticus is named); and *Jesus Barabbas*—the prisoner ironically released in place of *Jesus of Nazareth;* and there is another New Testament figure, *Jesus Justus* (Col. 4: 11).

So, first, the name of Jesus reminds us of the incarnation, the fact that God came as a human being and was given a human name typical of the context and culture in which he lived.

And secondly, it reminds us of the vocation of Jesus: 'He will save his people from their sins' (Matthew 1: 21). God saves. In Jesus Christ, God is delivering us from the power of darkness and reconciling us to himself.

Jesus, Saviour: when we invoke this name, we invoke the salvation of God himself. So, in the name of Jesus, we are pointed both to the human and the divine.

As the second chapter of Philippians reminds us, Jesus encapsulates the action of God, who in Jesus humbly comes to where we are, and to the very depths, to take us to the very heights.

Therefore God has highly exalted him and given him the name above all names; that at the name of Jesus every knee should bow.... and every tongue confess that Jesus Christ is Lord, to the glory of God the Father.

The name of Jesus reminds us that we inherit from Judaism an understanding of God as one who comes to his people in their need.

In Exodus Chapter 3, at the theophany of the Burning Bush, God reveals himself to Moses as a 'present' God, a God present in the history of his people:

I am the God of your father, the God of Abraham, the God of Isaac, and the God of Jacob.

and present also in the 'now' of his people's need:

I have observed the misery of my people... I have heard their cry... I know their sufferings, and I have come down to deliver them...

God sees, hears, knows and comes. This is the character of the God of the Exodus, and it is the character of the God who comes in Jesus to effect the new Exodus through the death and resurrection of his incarnate Son. The God of the Old Testament is a God who is characteristically present with and to his people, even though he is also a God who is holy, other, beyond, transcendent. The name of Jesus reminds us that this same God is actively present to save his people from their sins. In Jesus, God is not acting out of character, but is revealing and incarnating his very nature. *Emmanuel*, 'God with us', is another name of the human Jesus, and by invoking the name of Jesus we acknowledge and hallow the very name of God.

The Jesus Prayer, in its simplest form, is the naming of Jesus, a steady repetition of the name itself in quiet and loving attention: 'Jesus, Jesus, Jesus'. The one praying brings to this attentive repetition all that he or she knows and loves and trusts in the Saviour. The faithful reading of the Gospel stories and study of the teaching of the rest of the New Testament, the sharing in the life of the whole body of Christ in common worship and fellowship and mission, all add to the knowledge, not only of who Jesus is, but of Jesus as friend, Saviour and Lord in personal relationship and communion. The name is repeated in love and trust and in hope of eternal life in and through Jesus, who is the way, the truth and the life.

This is the heart of the Jesus Prayer. However much we add to it, this centre cannot be omitted, and it is the key that makes sense and prayer of however and wherever the Jesus Prayer is used.

* * * * * * *

In a time of quiet, try repeating slowly and attentively, simply the name of 'Jesus'. Let the repetition find its own rhythm.

e.g. with your breathing,

or to the rhythm of a favourite melody,

or perhaps on a 'prayer walk' to the rhythm of your steps.

JESUS IS LORD

Becoming Disciples

The heart of the Prayer, as we have seen, is the name of Jesus. The longer forms have developed not to distract from this but to assist our attention toward that centre. Each of the titles, Lord, Christ, Son of God, gives us insights into the ways in which the first followers and disciples related to Jesus of Nazareth. As we do theology, or Christology, by exploring these titles, we open to ourselves ways of entering into relationship with the Lord Jesus, the Christ and the Son of God; ways of *knowing* Jesus as the Way to the Father.

'Lord' is a word somewhat alien to the world of the late twentieth and early twenty-first centuries, and it is not easy to find any kind of contemporary parallel to speak to our anti-authority, anti-hierarchical culture. So rather than try, it may be better to make a leap of historical imagination and to think ourselves into the beginning of the Christian story.

In New Testament Greek, the title, *Kyrios—the Lord*, and the address, *Kyrie—Lord!* can simply be a term of ordinary respect, and in English versions is often translated appropriately as 'Sir'. As well as this simple term of respect, a more specific and direct relationship can be indicated:

As between Master and servant (*doulos*, 'slave')

Or between Teacher and disciple or student.

So sometimes our English versions will translate *Kyrios* or *Kyrie* as Lord or Master.[2]

In the secular Greek-speaking world, *Kyrios* would be used of a king or overlord or of anyone in authority. By the

---

[2] Behind the Greek of the New Testament documents, there is the spoken Aramaic, the first language of Jesus and of contemporary Jews. Jesus was sometimes addressed as *Rabbi*, teacher, or, as by Mary Magdalen, in the more intimate form of *Rabboni*.

11

close of the first century, the Roman Emperor eventually took the Latin title of *'Dominus et Deus'*, ('Our Lord and God'); so there is a sense in which, in the gentile world, *Kyrie, Kyrios*, had divine associations in some contexts.

In the world of Greek-speaking Jews this divine dimension was also latent, in that *Kyrios* had been used in the Greek version of the Hebrew scriptures (the Septuagint) to translate the Hebrew *Adon, Adonai,* 'Lord'. In Jewish formal and liturgical use of the scriptures a tradition had developed whereby the name that God revealed to Moses as *YHWH* (usually rendered *Yahweh*) was felt to be too awesome and holy to pronounce or write, and the custom grew of substituting *Adonai,* 'Lord'. Thus, when *Kyrios* was used in the Septuagint, it took on some of the awesome, divine overtones of *Adonai.* So the very title, *Kyrie,* as applied to Jesus was capable of carrying divine associations for anyone familiar with the Septuagint.

Exploring the various nuances of the title 'Lord' can be a way of exploring our own discipleship. We can imagine how, on first meeting Jesus in New Testament times *we* might first have addressed him as Lord, meaning little more than to show reverence toward someone who had been spoken of with respect.

We might also, as we grew to know more about him, have been aware of a compelling authority in the way he spoke and acted, and our respect would have deepened.

But not until we began to be challenged and inspired by his teaching would our use of the title 'Lord' imply any kind of personal relationship as of a student to teacher, and only as we became drawn into the community of disciples would we begin to share in relating to Jesus as servant to Master.

It seems from the Gospels that Jesus did indeed acknowledge this master-servant relationship with his followers, but he interpreted it very differently from the prevailing culture around him, teaching that the Lord and Master is to be servant to his people, even to wash their feet as the sign of his humble love for them.

As we grow in understanding of this relationship, the title 'Lord' begins to have a more profound and moving significance for us. There is something about *this* Lordship which gives us an amazing new insight into the nature of the compassionate and merciful God whom Jesus preaches and invites us to know.

As disciples we come to grasp, if only faintly, that we are in touch with the mystery of the Heavenly Father whom Jesus invites us to call 'Abba'. We are amazed, and yet not amazed, when Jesus says, 'No-one comes to the Father except by me', and again, 'Anyone who has seen me has seen the Father', for being with Jesus has drawn aside a curtain; we have been in touch with divine mysteries in our relationship with the one we now call 'Lord'. All this has prepared us to recognize in the risen Christ someone in whom God has spoken and is present. And with Thomas, we too can say, 'My Lord and my God!'

There is one further step into the mystery of this deepening relationship. There is in the New Testament a sprinkling of words from the Aramaic language which Jesus would have spoken. I have mentioned *Rabbi*, and *Rabboni*; also *Abba*; others are *ephatha*, 'be opened'; *talitha cum*, 'little girl, get up'; and there is also *Amen, Amen*, which seems to have been a characteristic idiom of Jesus as he announced some solemn truth. Another word is the prayer used in the book of Revelation and in I Cor. 16: 22—*Maranatha*, 'our Lord, come'.

It seems that where Aramaic words or phrases have been preserved in New Testament Greek, it probably indicates that a much loved or often repeated prayer or story is so precious that the original spoken sound has been cherished and held onto by the early Christian communities.

Maranatha, meaning 'Our Lord, come!' expresses the faith and hope and love, perhaps of early, persecuted Christians, and reveals the depth of meaning for the Church of the title 'Lord'. The beloved Teacher and Master, with whom the disciple has formed a reverent and intimate relationship and communion, is to be at last welcomed back in all his divine glory at the last day:

Maranatha. Amen; 'Come Lord Jesus'.

'No one can say "Jesus is Lord", except by the Holy Spirit.' This is the teaching of Paul in I Cor. 12: 3. In the Jesus prayer, as we repeat the words 'Lord, Jesus' with loving attention, we are already caught up and enfolded in the mystery of the God who is Father, Son and Holy Spirit, and as we look at the further titles, 'Christ' and 'Son of God', we shall begin to see why teachers of the prayer claim that it contains the whole mystery of the Christian faith.

* * * * * * *

In a time of quiet, try using simply the two words,

'Lord, Jesus',

repeating them to whatever is a helpful rhythm for you.

14

CHRIST THE KING

Jesus, the anointed, the Messiah, the Christ

'Lord Jesus Christ, Son of God'.... The first part of the full Jesus Prayer as yet contains no petition, and can be prayed simply as attentive and adoring invocation of the name. As we explore the title 'Christ', we can further enrich our understanding of the relationship we have to the one we worship.

The title 'Christ' is so often used in ordinary speech as if it is a sort of surname, but it is, of course, the Greek form of the Hebrew title 'Messiah', meaning 'the Anointed', and in the Hebrew Scriptures the title 'God's Anointed' could apply to priest or king.

Anointing with oil is a custom alien to our North European modern culture, except as used in rituals like a coronation, or in church initiation rites (each presumably dependent on older or biblical traditions). Church members may also be familiar with the use of oil as a sign of the ministry of healing.

Brought up in a modern industrial society, my first association with oil was the rather nasty black marks caused if one rubbed one's clothes against a bicycle chain! And in my childhood, things like salad oil, or nice smelling bath oils were not part of daily experience. So when I came across, for instance, psalm 133, and the words,

> How very good and pleasant it is
>   when kindred live together in unity!
> It is like the precious oil on the head,
>   running down upon the beard,
> on the beard of Aaron,
>   running down over the collar of his robes.

I felt rather physical discomfort at the thought of nasty sticky trickles going down the neck! If I had been brought up in a hot dry climate, and experienced the luxury of dry skin being massaged with moisturising and aromatic oils, I might have reacted differently.

In Matthew 6 we read that Jesus taught:

> And whenever you fast, do not look dismal, like the hypocrites, for they disfigure their faces so as to show others that they are fasting. …. But when you fast, put oil on your head and wash your face, so that your fasting may be seen not by others but by your Father ….

It seems that, as in many hot countries today, oil poured on the head was a normal refreshing toilet, so the ritual use of oil comes from a very positive context, in which to anoint someone was to honour them with a respectful and attentive service.

John Eaton gives a beautiful insight into the priestly anointing in his commentary on Ps. 133:

> This wonderful gift (of unity) for which the pilgrims longed, is first compared with the sacramental oil (Ex. 30. 23f.) used to install Aaron as the archetypal high priest; it was poured over his head and ran down his beard and over his vestments (themselves symbolic of the twelve tribes, Ex. 28. 9f). This aromatic oil was a sign of the holy power of God passing down upon the representative figure of Aaron.[3]

The first kings of Israel were anointed ritually by the prophet Samuel on behalf of the Lord. It is interesting that kings in the early history of Israel always had something of a priestly function. They stood before God on behalf of the nation, authorised to offer sacrifice on behalf of the people and having an up-front role in the liturgy of temple worship; they also lived almost literally in the house of God, the royal palace being adjacent to and integrally part of the Temple complex.

---

[3] John Eaton, *The Psalms: A Historical and Spiritual Commentary*, (Continuum Biblical Studies), 2003, p.446.

The Old Testament is ambivalent about its kings because only God can be truly the King of his people. Human kingship, as idealised stories of David and the texts of many of the psalms illustrate, implied humility and representative suffering on behalf of the people. In practice, of course, this did not prevent kings acting in autocratic ways, but the ideal is preserved in prophecies about the Messiah, the anointed of God. The shortcomings of earthly kingship, and indeed of earthly priesthood, would one day be transcended by the one who would truly be the Lord's anointed, the Messiah, or, in Greek, the Christ.

In New Testament theology, Jesus, son of David, fulfils the role of the Lord's anointed, the Messiah. In his person he takes on the suffering of his people, standing before God on their behalf and announcing in word and action the Reign of God. We read too in Luke 4: 18 that Jesus is anointed to be liberator and saviour, to preach the good news and 'to proclaim the acceptable year of the Lord'.

Jesus, it seems, was unwilling to accept the title of Messiah in his lifetime, probably because the current expectation was of a warrior/liberator who would restore the Davidic kingdom to Israel. Jesus never understood his own vocation in this way, and when Peter named him as the Christ, while not denying the truth, he forbade his disciples to spread this news. He immediately went on to teach of his vocation to suffer and be put to death; a destiny never directly foretold for the Messiah, though prophecy such as Deutero-Isaiah expressed insights into the truth of such a destiny for the representative 'Servant of God'.

Ironically, it is a criminal, crucified with Jesus, who recognizes the Kingship of Jesus in the midst of suffering and prays, 'Jesus remember me when you come into your kingdom'.

When we address Jesus as Christ, the title carries all these connotations of divinely ordained priesthood and kingship, representative suffering, fulfilment of the promises of deliverance and salvation; and further, it involves the followers of Christ in his ministry and destiny.

All four Gospels preserve the tradition that at the outset of his ministry Jesus received a mysterious anointing by God. In the story of the Baptism of Jesus, the God who is Father, Son and Spirit is graphically and mysteriously present. As Jesus rises from the waters of Baptism, the Spirit descends on him 'in the form of a dove' and a voice is heard, 'This is my son, the Beloved …'. There is the echo here of Psalm 2: 6, 7:

I have set my King on Zion, my holy hill. …He said to me, 'You are my Son, today I have begotten you.'

Because the King, the Christ, is understood as representative of his people, those who are followers of Jesus the Christ (as Paul's theology so often emphasizes) are baptised into Christ, baptised into the death and resurrection of Jesus, into the fellowship of Christ in his vocation and destiny. Being transferred into his kingdom, Christians share in his anointing and in his ministry.

To pray to Jesus as the Christ, then, is to become caught up in the life of the Messiah, the King. The prayer becomes one of commitment to our vocation, as we put our trust in Jesus as Lord and Christ and acknowledge the significance of our own baptism, our own anointing into the pattern of his ministry.

* * * * * *

In a time of quiet, try repeating the words:

'Lord, Jesus, Christ: Lord, Jesus, Christ'

or sing (aloud or in your heart) the Taizé chant:

'O Christe Domine Jesu'.

SON OF GOD

The presence of the Trinity in the Jesus Prayer

Classical and orthodox authorities on the Jesus Prayer seem to recommend that, though there are different forms of the prayer, varying in length from one word, 'Jesus', to the full form, 'Lord Jesus Christ, Son of God, have mercy on me a sinner', a single, consistent form should be chosen by the one practising the prayer rather than a flexible use of different forms at different times. One exception I have noticed is that when using the prayer as intercession for another, we are directed not to add the words 'a sinner'; this should only be used as denoting oneself—a wise and understandable exception!

As an amateur, not having any personal, authoritative director, I have found that it has not been helpful to stick rigidly to this advice; on the contrary, I have found myself led to vary my use of the prayer. This may be a matter of temperament, and hopefully other amateurs will find what is right and fruitful for them. I normally use the full form of the prayer but often approach or lead up to this practice by using simply the first half of the prayer, up to and including the title 'Son of God'.

I find that using this first half of the prayer directs my attention to the person of Jesus in adoration and worship without any form of petition which brings attention back to my own needs. I can simply rest in the truth that Jesus *is*, and in the wonder of *who* Jesus is, and allow that truth and that wonder to be a window into the mystery of the Trinity.

When repeating the whole prayer, I have also found it fruitful sometimes to vary the emphasis of attention: at times to the name 'Jesus'; at times to the title, 'Lord'; or to 'Christ, Son of God'.

It is not a matter of stopping to think about the meaning, but of allowing short insights, such as those touched on in this series of reflections, to light up the whole prayer or to beckon the attention back to the subject. It's a bit like a touch on the steering wheel when a learner driver finds herself inadvertently steering in the direction of something noticed on the side of the road!

The title 'Son of God' is an important part of the theology of the prayer. I have said that the name 'Jesus' is the heart of the prayer, and that remains so for me, however I vary the use of the prayer. The phrase 'Son of God', however, in terms of rhythm and of length is at the centre. For me this is helpful in that it keeps me aware of the implicit presence of God as Trinity—Father, Son and Spirit—even though the words are *explicitly* addressed to Jesus.

> God has sent the Spirit of his Son into our hearts, crying 'Abba! Father!'
>
> Galatians 4: 6

Somehow, implicitly as I acknowledge and worship Jesus as Son of God, I am also crying out in my heart to God as Father. I am co-operating in my prayer with the dynamic of that movement:

> ... it is that very Spirit bearing witness with our spirit that we are children of God ....
>
> Romans 8: 16

Like the title 'Christ', the words 'Son of God' direct us to the Baptism of Jesus, the anointing of the Spirit and the witness of the voice from heaven, 'this is my Son, my beloved'.

In Acts 10: 38, Peter's sermon to Cornelius includes the comment:

> God anointed Jesus of Nazareth with the Holy Spirit and with power; ...

In both Christian art and in liturgical traditions, the Baptism of Jesus is seen as a theophany, a revealing of God as Father, Son and Spirit. Another Gospel theophany is the Transfiguration, where the three disciples hear from the cloud the words, 'This is my Son, my Beloved; listen to him'. Here the Father directs the disciples to his Son, commanding attentive *obedience* to his words. 'Listen', in the Hebrew scriptures, implies obedience; to 'hear the word of the Lord' means *doing* what God commands. The disciples are invited into the 'abba' relationship of the beloved Son to his Father.

> Jesus said to them, 'Very truly, I tell you, the Son can do nothing on his own, but only what he sees the Father doing.'
> John 5: 19

> He said, 'Abba, Father, for you all things are possible; remove this cup from me; yet not what I want, but what you want.'
> Mark 14: 36

We are invited *into* this relationship of obedience, as we pray to Jesus as Son of God, listening to him as we attend to him in our prayer. The Jesus Prayer brings us into the teaching of Jesus who said, 'When you pray, say "Father"...' It can be a way of communion with the Son which, through the Spirit in our hearts, draws us into his own trusting and obedient relationship with God as Father.

* * * * * * * *

In a time of quiet, try beginning to pray by using only the first half of the prayer, with emphasis of attention on the phrase,

'Son of God',

'Lord, Jesus, Christ, Son of God'.

21

MERCY

The Character of God

Behind the English word 'mercy' is the Greek word *eleos*. The English word, both liturgically and in secular contexts, is so often associated with the concept of forgiveness that we have frequently lost sight of the truth that in the Bible its meaning is much larger and only rarely refers to the overlooking or putting away of sin. For instance, the Greek word *eleos* is related to *elaion* (oil), which links, as does the word 'Christ', with the anointing which soothes and heals. In Jesus's parable where the traveller was attacked by thieves, the Samaritan pours wine and oil on the wounds for healing.

Behind the Greek words *eleos* and *eleison*, 'be merciful' or 'have mercy', is the Hebrew word *hesed*. This is a very beautiful and central word in Old Testament theology and worship. It is a frequent word in the psalms and is variously translated in our English versions as 'mercy, loving-kindness, steadfast love, faithful love, covenant love'.

The last variant is important and indicates the origin of the concept. *Hesed* is firstly that quality in God which can be trusted in and relied on because that is essentially his nature—faithfulness, steadfast love. But it has also the more intimate association of God's loving relationship with his chosen people, the people with whom he has made covenant.

So when God is asked to be merciful, to have mercy, he is not being asked to change his outlook, but to be himself, to act in character and according to the covenant agreement he himself initiated. In contrast, we hear the word 'mercy' used in some secular contexts where there is a plea for a change of heart; ruthless kidnappers are pleaded with to show mercy; a tyrannical despot is asked to be merciful to captives. This is not the spirit in which we seek mercy from God or from his Son, Jesus.

Sometimes even our liturgical traditions can obscure the confidence we should have in the merciful nature of God. For instance, the ancient *Kyrie eleison* prayer is often sung with subdued reticence rather than with joyful confidence; but at least the response often used for intercessory petitions, 'Lord in your mercy, hear our prayer', has familiarised us with a wider use of the word than in penitential contexts.

So in the Jesus Prayer, unless we use the longer form including the words 'on me, a sinner', there need be no explicit reference to penitence and forgiveness in the prayer: 'Lord, Jesus Christ, Son of God, have mercy on me'.

Of course, in all our approach to God, we need only have some small awareness of his majesty and overwhelming goodness to remember that we fall short, we are not worthy. So the prayer for God to show his faithful love will probably always, in this life, be tinged with the knowledge of our need for reconciliation and forgiveness. But the word 'mercy' shouldn't be reduced to this meaning alone.

As we pray 'Lord, Jesus Christ, Son of God, have mercy', not only for ourselves but in intercession for those we care about, for the needs of the church and of the world, the prayer begins to be a communication, a communion with the one who, in a new covenant, looks with enduring love upon his people and calls us to take our part in the outworking of that love through sharing in his own ministry of intercessory prayer, asking for mercy in the name of Jesus.

So if the name of Jesus is the heart of the prayer, the petition 'have mercy' is the pivot. The prayer begins with adoring attention to the truth of who Jesus is and the wonder of the presence of the Trinity as we pray, but then it is good to allow the petition 'have mercy' to surge up from the depths of that knowing of who Jesus is. To say 'Jesus, have mercy' is to acknowledge that I seek in Jesus the faithful, enduring, steadfast, covenant love of the Father. At times when we need a very short prayer, the words 'Jesus, mercy' or 'Jesus, have mercy' contain the whole prayer, and importantly can be a means of the transformation of our inner being.

If the Hebrew word *hesed* is central to the Old Testament, it is therefore part of the heritage of Jesus and of his disciples, 'Be merciful, just as your Father is merciful.' (Luke 6: 36); 'Blessed are the merciful, for they will receive mercy' (Matthew 5: 7).

Here we have the Hebrew understanding of how *hesed* works. Those who act mercifully, with constant love, in their daily lives, are reflecting the very nature of the God who acts mercifully and with faithful love toward his covenant people. To be transformed into the likeness of God is the vocation and destiny of God's 'New Covenant' people.

The mystics teach that we become like what we constantly contemplate. In Jesus we see the mercy and loving kindness of God:

> And all of us, with unveiled faces, seeing the glory of the Lord as though reflected in a mirror, are being transformed into the same image from one degree of glory to another; ...
>
> II Cor. 3: 18

To move, then, with the words 'have mercy', from attentive adoration of who Jesus is, into a prayer of petition, is to begin to co-operate consciously with this work of transformation in our hearts. The prayer changes key, and we are lifted into another dimension of its dynamic. We open ourselves to the transforming action of the one to whom we relate in prayer. We become exposed to the touch of God by our own consent, as it were. We are saying a kind of 'Amen' or 'yes' to the potentially transforming and therefore dangerous waters into which we were plunged at our baptism and by which we are united to the death, the resurrection and the high-priestly ministry of Christ who ever lives to make intercession for us (Heb. 7: 25). Our discipleship is our growing into the reality of that baptism into Christ, whose awesome vocation and destiny we have contemplated as we have named Jesus as Lord and Christ and Son of God. We now pray to be caught up into that vocation, as we say,

'Lord Jesus Christ, Son of God, have mercy on me.'

* * * * * * *

In a time of quiet, pray gently the two words:

'Jesus, mercy',

allowing this to expand to:

'Lord, Jesus, Christ, Son of God, have mercy.'

EARTHEN VESSELS

The treasury of God

> For it is the God who said, 'Let light shine out of darkness', who has shone in our hearts to give the light of the knowledge of the glory of God in the face of Jesus Christ. But we have this treasure in clay jars, so that it may be made clear that this extraordinary power belongs to God and does not come from us.
>
> II Cor. 4: 6-7.

Our vocation and our destiny is to become transformed into the likeness of Christ to be 'Christians', anointed children of God, and in Christ to reflect God's likeness and glory. But this treasure is, for the time being, in what Paul calls clay jars—or, as the older English versions translate, earthen vessels.

The beauty of this image is that the clay pots he refers to are the normal containers and preservers of precious things, treasures. We, you and I, are earthy, human, made of clay, the dust of the earth.

The word humility is based on a Latin root meaning earth—we have it in our gardening term, 'humus'. But it is this very earthiness, humanness, which *contains* the treasure! So when in the Jesus Prayer we confess ourselves as sinners, we are not meant to grovel and beat ourselves about the head. It is inevitable that clay will fall short of the glory of God, yet it *contains* that treasure. To sin is to fall short, miss the mark. We will all do that. Julian of Norwich has a teaching about sin which seems both mysterious and shocking. 'Sin is behovely,' she says, 'and all shall be well': 'behovely', meaning something like needful, or necessary, or we might interpret 'inevitable'.

To pray the Jesus prayer with its longer ending is not about being morbidly introspective. To pray 'have mercy on me a sinner' is a way of expressing our aspiration to be changed from glory to glory.

In the light of the face of Jesus Christ, we cannot but be aware of how we fall short, of how we fail to be merciful as our Father is merciful—merciful in constant, faithful loving kindness to one another and to *ourselves*. Unkindness to myself is no way to grow in mercy. But to speak of myself as a sinner is not unkind, but realistic. It opens the way for me to receive not only God's mercy but my own—to be patient with myself, my failings, my falling short of the standards I set for myself, which may not be the standards *God* sets for me!

This mercy to myself is what sets me free to love others, to be merciful in my attitude to others; for self-forgiveness includes the acknowledgement: 'Yes! That is what I am like!', and it makes me less surprised, less shocked, less judgmental about the failings of others.

The beauty of the Jesus Prayer is that it is a prayer for beginners. The acknowledgement of myself as a sinner is always a place for beginning again. It is the prayer of the disciple, the one growing into relationship with Jesus, and as a learner bound to make mistakes. However awesome the destiny of the one baptised into the death and resurrection of Christ, and however wondrous the vision of the glory of God in the face of Jesus Christ, the mercy of God is shaped always to deal with the clay of our humanness. This is a prayer which is both wide enough to hold us in the greatness of God's mercy, and small enough to be contained in the earthen vessel of our frail human lives, which constantly fall short and need to come back and begin again.

Each time we begin again, we come into the inner room of our hearts (see Matthew 6: 6), and through Jesus, Saviour, pray to our Father in secret. We are not leaving outside those bits of ourselves which make us sad or ashamed. We bring in with us our frailty, our incompleteness, and our constant failure to live the life of the merciful toward those who are close to us and those who, though far off, are also our neighbours. We bring our darker self into the room of prayer and expose it to the light of God's mercy to us in Jesus Christ.

So the 'Jesus prayer', the prayer of the heart, can be one of the ways that God can begin to transform our lives, make us like Jesus, recreate us in his own image and likeness. Then, in Christ, we in turn may be instruments of his mercy, his faithful loving-kindness toward humankind.

* * * * * * *

In a time of quiet, find a rhythm for yourself which includes the complete form of the Jesus Prayer, perhaps by breathing in for the first half:

'Lord Jesus Christ, Son of God,'

and breathing out for the petition:

'have mercy on me, a sinner.'